D0296962

911200003916 84

# KIDS WRITE JOKES

## 100% NONSENSE
## 254% HILARIOUS

BLINK

bringing you closer

Published by Blink Publishing
2.25, The Plaza,
535 Kings Road,
Chelsea Harbour,
London, SW10 0SZ

www.blinkpublishing.co.uk

facebook.com/blinkpublishing
twitter.com/blinkpublishing

Hardback — 978-1-78870-057-3
Ebook — 978-1-78870-058-0

A CIP catalogue of this book is available from the British Library.

Typset by Envy Limited
Printed and bound by Stige Arti Grafiche

1 3 5 7 9 10 8 6 4 2

Blink Publishing is an imprint of Bonnier Books UK
www.bonnierbooks.co.uk

For Molly,
the funniest one of all

# Introduction

Once upon a time, the company I worked for launched a website for kids' jokes, and — fortunately for me — I was given the task of reviewing the jokes that were sent in.

It became clear that children often have a very special view on what constitutes a 'joke': they don't have to actually make any sense.

At all.

While I sat there at my desk moderating submissions, I started to realise that a lot of the 'incorrect' jokes I was rejecting were actually funnier than the ones I was letting through. Many of them made me laugh out loud in the office. I decided that the world deserved to share in that laughter, and my Tumblr account for Bad Kids Jokes was born.

It didn't take long for the online community to discover the content and, quite frankly, to go a bit crazy over it. And then the press got interested: *The Times*, *Huffington Post*, *Rolling Stone*, Mashable and BuzzFeed all wrote articles about the site. *The Independent* published a story in the newspaper about it. It was mentioned on BBC Radio. Oh, plus Stephen Colbert and Sarah Silverman read some of the jokes out on The Late Show.

Thrilled and amazed by the response, I relaunched the content on Twitter as Kids Write Jokes, and it turns out that tens of thousands of people agree with me that the 'jokes' are hilarious.

Why is it so popular? I think it's the fact that every time you read one of these jokes, you picture a young child writing it, convinced and excited that they have something hilarious and amazing to share. The childhood innocence of silly nonsense is universally enjoyable. Sometimes the kids forget that jokes need a punchline. Sometimes they randomly miss out a key point that would have made the whole thing work. And sometimes they forget that a joke needs to be, well, a joke. But to the kid writing it, it makes perfect sense, and that's what's so funny about them and why I love these jokes so much. It's also why I've left each one untouched and unedited — here for the first time in this book in their original form!

I hope you have as much fun reading these as I did compiling them. I still laugh out loud as I read through these pages.

@KidsWriteJokes

why was the naked man naked.

a. he had nakedpower.

b. he had a naked pecan friend.

c. he was naked man.

(james, 8)

A duck walks into a bar. A man runs out because its unnatural to have a duck in a bar.

why the man was naked
a. he was naked lad
b. he had a buttcheek
c. buttoast

(james, 8)

Why do fish have hands?
because they don't have hands

Im going to get to the BOTTEM
of this.
HA HA HA HA HA HA HA HA HA HA HA
HA HA HA HA HA HA HA HA HA HA HA
HA HA HA HA HA HA HA HA HA HA HA
HA HA HA HA HA HA HA HA HA HA HA
HA HA HA HA HA HA HA HA HA.

Doctor Doctor I feel like im a curtain

Shut Up

a man found a raisin in the woods.
"what a funny looking raisin."
"im not a raisin im just an ant
with no legs."

What did the goat say to the dog
nice buttock you loser

KNOCK KNOCK! WHOS THERE.
REX THE DUMPLING EGG

doctor doctor i fell over
get back up then cheese face

what is furry and lays eggs
and also flys?
a hot air chicken egg

doctor: u look look like the walking dead

man: i just have a cold

doctor: oh yeh, im not a doctor, im a builder

guess what the chicken was wearing

**monkey pants**

docter docter i have worms in my garden
i dont care cant you see im busy
you are doing youre nails.

(seth, 8)

What does your mum need to make
her fase very dirtey
SHE needs to go in the bin
47484474747474747474474747474
times

how meny kicks dus it take to
brake a bed
1000

why did the man scream
his pet chiken pooped on his
computer

(holly)

how do you lose four pounds

*cut your hed off*

I have a butt
Sir we all have butts

knock knock
toilet to the rescue

what do you call a donkey with a
millon eyes and a millon legs.
a monster

(rose, 7)

what is crazy and funny
a monkey on a windmill

(melissa)

why did the frog cross the rode ?

to get a new tong

why ?

because it's tong was stuck to a

velkro tree

how?

the tree was coverd in syrip

what flavor?

mint

**LETS SEE WHAT DO WE HAVE HERE**
**A POO**

Why does mums get so angry
because when she sends you to your
rhoom she can read a fashion book

If a wookie get shot and
it suvives is it a lucky wookie

Knock, knock
who's there?
Posh
Posh who?
Posh lady, bye I have to go and
shop i need more hats


there was two fish in a tank and
one of the fish said
do you know how to drive this thing
**BECAUSE THE FISH ARE DRIVEING**
**THE TANK IN A WAR**

what did the floor say to the chair

get off me u fat idiot

if you want to catch a bear in the
winter you cut a hole in the ice then
put peas around it then when he comes
to eat them kick him in the ice hole

Q. Doctor doctor I feel like a spoon
A. well stop looking at spoons

(Harriet!)

what do you call a pig with ears?
dum head

wat do you coll a spider with no legs.
a hairy piece of trash !!!!!!!!!!!!

Once aponer time
The end
HAHAHAHAHAHAHAH

it was a dark and creepy night
there was a black and white figure in
the forest
it was a cow

the duck went into the farmers house
duck: can i have some bread
farmer: no
duck: can i have some bread
farmer: no
duck: can i have some bread
farmer: **FOR THE LAST TIME NO**

i appear once in a second, twice in a month and three times in a year, what am i
dont bother theres no answer.

what do you call a deer with no eyes ears mouth and legs?
**NO I DEER**

(jack)

why was a chiken very cross
with the pig
because he lade 100000 eggs and he
was tired and the pig dident do the
tidying up.

knock knock
whos there
i eat trash
i eat trash who
give me some money thats who

(ryan)

what do you call a sandwitch
with legs
**bready legs**

**WHAT DO YOU DO IF A DINASUAR
LOVES YOU
YOU HIDE**

what did the egg say to the other egg?
have a eggsellent day.
i hope you laugh out loud and tell
your friends this joke. if your friends
dont get the joke explain the joke.
IT WILL BE FUNNY

what do you call a fish with no legs
a fsh

(Aurora D)

Q. what did the cheese say to the moldy cheese?

A. you look unwell i will take you to Dr cheese

(josh)

DINOSAUR JOKE

KNOCK KNOCK

WHO'S THERE

DINO

DINO WHO

DINOSAUR

why did the cow stare at the orange
juice for three hours
because it said stare

Teacher: Did you ever hear the story of the orange

Child: No

Teacher: aw too bad

what did the doctor say to the
platypus?
you sir are in quite a pickle

man: waiter how long will my pizza be?

waiter: not very long. lol

how do you get?

put it in a bag whith water and put it on the floor

hahahaha
**NOTHING!**

how do you talk to a doctor
in posh language

waiter do you have frog legs.
no Ive always had ketchup legs
with poo on them.

(olly)

what did the muscleman say
to the tiger

ooooooooooooooooooooooooooooo
ooooooooooooooooooooooooooooo
oooooooooooooooo.

a man goes to the doctor and said
"doctor I think I have something
stuck in my throught"
so the doctor said "let's take a x-ray"
(this doctor did not no about spines)
"i see the problem a bone is there"

what dose a acid monster have
for lunch?
a acid sandwich

knock knock
whose there
boiled
boiled who
eggs

What do you call a dinosaur
with no eyes?
Shut up

knock knock
who is there
boss
boss who
boss will you give me some pens

(m harris, 7)

doctor doctor i think i am a spoon.
sit on that chair and stop staring.

(ella bella)

WHAT DO U CALL A FREAK HORSE
**JESSICA**

if you go to the ham contest wat
will the man say
you won last year you are
not alowed

well well well. your JUST IN TIME

**Question:** What do you call a lady with a lady with marmelade on her head.

**Answer:** Margret.

why did the chiken running around screming
because it needed to use the toilot

gess how many snakes there are
13

what do you call a camel with no
bones in his back
a horse

what do you call a monkey
eating keys?
bonkers

IGLOO YOUR NOT FUNNY DO YOU UNDERSTAND

crocodiles might be vegitarians because when they open their mouths, we could easily put in vegetables!

why do old people use a walking stick?
because they like colecting sticks.

what did the orange do in the tree?
orange business

Q:What do you call a dog that can walk?

A:A HUMAN.

what do you call a person who is yellow?
a cheese statue

(taylor)

Knock knock
whos there
BOB HUMBUG
Bob Humbug who
naughty bob humbug


docter docter i hit my head
what do you want me to do stupid

the lady went down to the BOTOM
of a mountain
lol

were did the ghost watch tv all night.
in his haunted casle

what do cavemen eat

caves

what do you call a pig that does
kararty
**kararty pig man**

what is funny and has eight legs
a clown

what do spys eat instead of
mcdonalds?
spydonalds

bob: doctor doctor i need
a new but.
doctor: what is it bob.
bob: it has a crack in it
doctor: that is normal bob

what did the rabit say to the goat
oi stop messing up my house

(ben)

mum: there are worms in my plate

waiter: those are sousages

what do you call a tiger with
glasses on?
a scientist tiger

wats the difrent btween a cat
and a frog
thay ony have 10 legs

(rahul, 6)

the pig walked into the shop and
the lady said we dont make types of
meat in this shop

the other day i met a man called smith and i said whats the name of his other leg

WHAT DID THE MAN SAY TO THE CURTAIN WHEN IT KEPT CHATTING? SHUT UP LOL

if mr brown lived in the brown house
and mr purple lived in the purple
house who lives in the white house
the mayor

**What goes on the motor way at 90 miles an hour?**
**a baked bean in a jug**

how does a poo get out of the toilet?
**somhow**

(sammi)

what do you call a vampire with
2 trousers?
**double trousers**

what is yellow black and orange?
a newspaper

what is a thunder cats favrite food?
chips and poo and toilets

this boy went to school, his teacher asked him "whats your name?" the boy said "i don't know". so that day he went to his mother and said "whats my name?" so she said cant you see that im tidying up!!!

(nandita, 7)

Q) why did'nt the man clime up the mountain

A) because there wasn't a mountain

knock
how there
duck
duck who
chicken legs

what is brown and slow and an animal?

**A BROWN CHIPMUNK OLD GRANNY**

(isabel, 7)

what do get when you cross a vampire,
homework and brusel sprouts
i dont know its probalely super
dangerous

*(alex, 8)*

WHY DID THE BANANA CROSS THE ROAD.
TO FIND BANANA SANTA IN BANANA
LAND WITH BANANA UNDERPANTS

*(BETHANY R)*

# What person just talks and talks and talks

## A TEACHER !!!!

*(Kaleigh, 9)*

why was the hen walking on its head?
BECAUSE IT HAD A HEMERGENCY

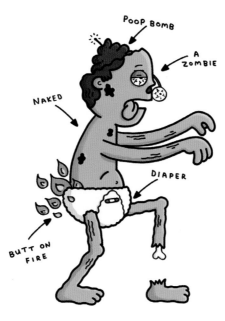

Your brain is a poop bomb and you
are a zombie and you are naked with
your butt on fire and your butt in a
girls face and you are wearing diapers

why did the cow poo on the man?
a man has a toilet but a cow dose'nt.
so a man is a cows toilet

what would you call a man
with no head?
a non head

(matthew, 7)

what do you get when you cross a centerpede and a pig?
bacon legs

what is the capital of egg.
York

*(Sara)*

Q. whats worse than getting back a test with a zero?

A. getting back a test with 100%. brag about it. quit from school. then find out it wasent really yours. you got zero.

# Whats day is March 27........
# St Fartpants Day.

why did tom and jerry get married
Because tom was a boy and jerry
was a boy and they were strong as a
toliet.

WHY WAS THE NINJA IN THE
KITCHEN?
YOU TELL ME!!!!!!!!!!!!!!!!!!!!!

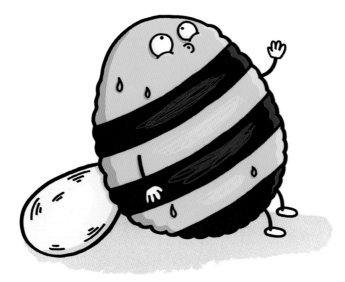

whats round fat and is sticky
a greedy bee

do you know one man asked his son
to bring eggs
but he broght apples

*(nath, 6)*

300 + 5967 - 400 + 20 = head ake

why did the chicken marry the crocodile

because crocodooladoo is good family name.

**whats ugly but happy
a frog**

Why does the chef always
be right........
Because he's the chef.

what do you call a deer with no eyes
EYE dunno

(sam, 7)

What is the secret ingrediant
of a toilot?
Poo

why did the cow go to the movies?
because movies

what makes a super hero fly?
hero dust . boring right

**WHERE DO CHIKENS GO AT THE WEEKEND**

**WEEKEND**

**THE MOVIES**

your a bin

no I m not

you look like one

ok I am

How do you get a tissue to dance?
You put a little boogie in it
(DONT TRY THIS AT HOME ANYBODY)

What does A friendly neighbor do to you?

1.Buy you a playStation 4.

2.He does'nt care when your stealing.

3.He gave you his credit card.

4.He's kind but he got nothing now.

what did the man do with time

**wasted it**

How do you hire a teddy bear?
Put him on stilts!
(if you don't get it hire as make tall
if you still don't get it sorry for the
inconvenience)

(Jackson, 9)

where do cows go on holiday
**FRANCE**

what is the best part of bread......
bread

what do call when two circles are
next to each other.
a butt

monkey joke

q: what keys cant you play on
a piano

a: a monkey

What did the flashlight say
to the car?

Stop it i am changing

Doctor doctor! I feel cold!

Then pull yourself togever man

(Lukas H)

why did mr potateo run from the
cops?
because he killed mrs carrot face and
robbed mr broccili pants.

Why does my uncle Kevin
have a run everyday
because he wants to have a
bit of "me" time

what has eight legs eight heads
and 8 arms
= 8 men

hello yes this is a prank call madam you have won 200,0000,000,00 million pounds!

knock knock
who is there
doctor smelly feet.

what's green and hangs off trees

**GIRAFFE**

why did the banana go to the
doctors?
why?
because he had kechup on he,s head.

What is pink, white and sits in corners while having pizza stuck on the top layered part of the skeleton protecting it outside?
A baby rat in a bag of salt with hot cheese on it's face!

why did the lady put ham in her hand bag ?
because someone told her it was a ham-bag.

A man of the chicken layed a egg on a pointy mountain. There was a big wind and the egg rolled down.
Where did the egg Fall?
The man of the chicken does not lay eggs!!!

(sophia)

why did the potato cross the road to get to the postbox

Dad what is the square root of 144?
WHO CARES!!?? YOU'RE GROUNDED!!!

why did the lion eat the snake
because it looked like a sausoge

Q: why do bees have black stripes
A: they live in the dark

(ava, 8)

what did a bee say to a other bee?
i love plants

why did the turkey go on the plane
to go to turkey

*(ffion, 7)*

what do you call a fish with no tail?

a one eyed grape

why didn't the skeleton go swimming
because his eyeballs will be filled
with water

Q. Why are Zombies fast
A. To catch the bus

what has 3 eyes 6 legs and 2 noses
a Cyclops goat with a man wearing
a animal suit breeding

What did the chicken say to the pilot?
Can I have a ride to chicken island.

Waiter waiter why is there a
foot on my cake
Because you told me to stamp on it

docter docter I feel like a bunch of curtans

then open them up

(marla, 7)

why is the mash potato not cool?
Because it isnt wearing sun glasses.

**WHAT DOES A MONKEY KEEP AS A SECRET**
**THAIR BANANAS**

what's a jedi's favorite food?
lightsaber casserole

Knock,Knock......
Who's There?.....
The Big Bad Wolf......
What Do You Want?.......
Coloured EGGS......
What colour?.......
RED!!!!!!!!!!!!!!!!!!!!!!!!!!!!!!!!

WHAT DOES PEAS EAT?

TOAST

Father: Shut up! Don't tell your father how to manage our business. I have eaten more salt than you have rice

why shoudnt you go to the fridge
without permition
**because it will come for its revenge**

"docter docter IVE EATEN TOO MUCH TRASHCAN SURPRISE"

"DONT TALK RUBISH"

knock knock
who's there
the guy who works all day
the guy who works all day who
i wake up i shower i go to work
i work all day i go home i sleep

A MAN ALWAYS LAUGHING HIS NAME IS WILLSON. 1 DAY A FREIND OF WILLSON ASK HIM:WHY YOU ALWAYS HAPPY? WILLSON LOOK HIM FREIND AND SLAP HIM FREIND AND THAT DAY WILLSON NEVER LAUGH BECAUSE WILLSON IS GHOST NOW

What do you call a fish with no eyes
fishhhhhhhhhhhhhhhhhh

A guy was at a shop he brought dome lobsters and said to the man: AAAAAGH its a crab. And the other man said thats not a crab its a orange pencil.

what do you say when somethig carnt fly?
can it fly yet

What do you call a ufo that
looks like a butt?
A buttfo

Q: Why is Birmingham called Birmingham?

A: Because they like to burn ham